A RIZVI FAMILY WINTER

First published in India by HarperCollins *Children's Books* 2025
An imprint of HarperCollins *Publishers*

HarperCollins Publishers India, Cyber City, Building 10-A,
Gurugram, Haryana-122002, India

www.harpercollins.co.in

2 4 6 8 10 9 7 5 3 1

P-ISBN: 978-93-6989-631-8
E-ISBN: 978-93-6989-710-0

Series design by Denise Antao
Layout and design in Quicksand 10pt/16 by Isha Nagar

Printed and bound at Thomson Press India Ltd

*

HarperCollins Publishers, Macken House, 39/40 Mayor Street Upper,
Dublin 1, D01 C9W8, Ireland

This book is produced from independently certified FSC® paper
to ensure responsible forest management.

A RIZVI FAMILY WINTER

SADAF SIDDIQUE

ILLUSTRATED BY
RIYA NAGENDRA

MUNEER RIZVI
NAZNEEN RIZVI
PARVEZ
PARVEEN
QAMAR
QAISAR
TANAAZ
SEHAR
UROOJ
VALI

RUKHSANA
RASHEED
OMAIR
WASIF
XENIA
SHARFU CHACHA

For my triple As – Atif, Arham and Aamna,
and all the wild, whacky adventures ahead!
Sadaf

To Brocci, my cantankerous wonder.
Riya

CHAPTER 1

December 15: Hope and Flying Slippers

'I don't want to go,' said Sehar.

'Neither do I,' I agreed.

Sehar and I never agree about anything but here we were, staring at our bags, hoping for a Christmas miracle to change our travel plans. The problem was Ammi said the tickets were non-refundable—and we don't celebrate Christmas.

But miracles? One can always hope.

See, Nana and Nani wanted the

whole family to join them this winter in Solan. I know what you are thinking—snow in Himachal! Family time! Ya, no. We aren't a family that likes cosy nights by the fireplace. Mostly because Nana's ancient fireplace is a fire hazard. Nana and Nani live by themselves—OK OK, Omair Mammu lives with them too—in an old rickety house in the hills.

You can see the three-storeyed house and its steepled, slate-tiled roof on the drive up the winding roads to the house. Nana's apple orchards are practically in the backyard. Really. You just walk out and pluck some rosy red apples. You can see the whole orchard from the terrace on the third floor. But wintertime means icy winding roads and no apple picking.

The last time we were there, all the kids were shoved into a room opposite the terrace, while the parents took over their old bedrooms. Qamar Khala's daughter Urooj and Sehar had a cold war after Urooj referred to Sehar's co-ord set as pyjamas. This year, Sehar turned the Big 13, which, in her mind, gave her the right to dismiss anyone who is not a teenager. Namely, the rest of us.

'How will I stay in touch with my friends?' she whined to Ammi.

'It's only for two weeks. I am sure they will survive.'

'Dia is going to London, and Arti's family is staying at a wildlife resort. Why can't we go somewhere fun for the holidays?'

'You'll see Solan in the winter, and you can find plenty of wildlife there too! Besides, it is the first time in a long time the whole family is going to be together,' Ammi replied, unmoved.

'So why do *we* have to suffer?' I said.

A poorly timed flying slipper whizzed past my ear.

'Spending time with family is fun!' Ammi retorted.

'Not with spotty wi-fi,' said Sehar.

'Or without my PS4. Or my friends. Or my karate class,' I sighed.

'R.I.P. us,' Sehar added.

I went to bed praying for a miracle, and woke up to Ammi screaming at everyone to get up or we would miss the plane.

Like I said, one can hope.

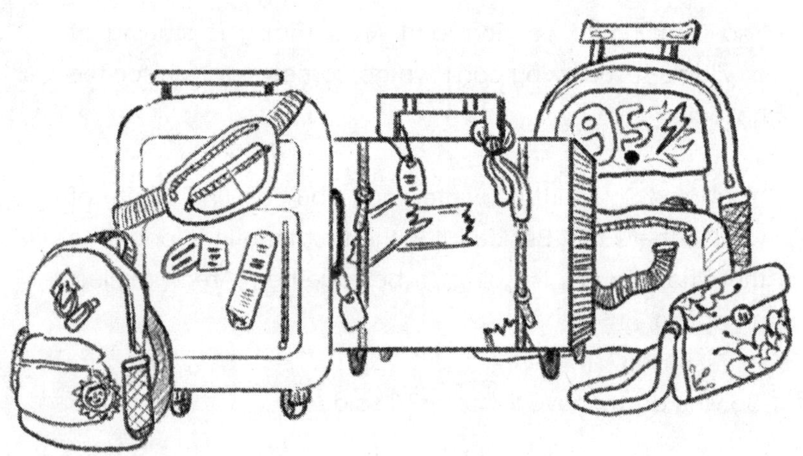

CHAPTER 2

December 16: Bump in the Night

All my hopes for a miracle flew out of the window as our taxi travelled through ribbons and ribbons of winding, twisting roads, which Sehar said twisted her insides. I suppose we were lucky she didn't spew out all the packets of Kurkure she had eaten along the way. While Ammi and Dad slept, I spent most of the trip pushing Sehar's head off my tired shoulders, until I fell asleep myself, squished against the window.

‘Wake up, sleeping beauty,’ called Sehar. ‘We are here.’

‘Naz Manzil’ came slowly into focus. With its dark timber windows, grey slated tiled roof and the Himalayas as a backdrop, it looked a pretty picture. A pretty isolated picture, I should say.

‘There she is, the Late Lateef!’ called out Omair Mammu, when he saw Ammi. ‘We thought you took a detour to Manila!’

‘Uff,’ said Qamar Khala, shaking her head, ‘Manali, not Manila.’

‘Hain, hain, same-same,’ said Omair Mammu, hugging Ammi. Ammi hugged Qamar Khala and Rukhsana Mammi till she finally reached Nana. ‘Salaam Abbu,’ she said. Nana returned her salaam and placed his hand on her head. Ammi locked her hand in his and they walked into the house together.

We salaam-ed our way in, one by one, following Ammi’s footsteps and were met with slaps on our backs and crushed by bear hugs. I spotted Vali in Nana’s study, his frizzy hair and eyeglasses peering over the top of a book.

‘Hii . . .’ I started to say, but then Rukhsana Mammi turned around whiplash fast. ‘I mean salaam Vali,’ I quickly corrected myself.

‘As’salaam Alaikum, Vali,’ Rukhsana Mammi said, correcting my correction.

‘Walaikum As’salaam. Did you know this house was earlier surrounded by a cemetery?’

‘Thanks for the creepy fact, Vali,’ I said as I backtracked . . . and bumped into Rasheed Mammu.

‘If it isn’t my little chipkali.’ Rasheed Mammu had given me this questionable nickname after our last visit, when I’d spent all my time hiding from Wasif’s seeking. But this time I was prepared. I hadn’t enrolled in martial arts just for kicks.

‘Oye, Tanaaz Toothpaste,’ said a loud voice from the staircase. Wasif raced down the stairs and slapped the back of my head. I ran after him through the kitchen, yelling quick salaams to Sharfu Chacha and nearly toppling a bubbling pot of what smelt like aloo gosht. The kitchen back door

opens out to Nana's apple orchards, filled with orderly lines of trees minus the famous Himalayan red apples. Though possibly now less famous than Himalayan pink salt.

We raced across the trees. I was slow, not used to being wrapped up in layers. Wasif was way ahead. I huffed and puffed and stopped for a second to catch my breath, only to see an arrow whizz past me and hit the trunk of an apple tree right near my head.

'Dang it!' came the unmistakable ring of Nani's voice. I should have guessed my archery-loving grandmother was practising out in the orchard. A quick glance showed me the target she was aiming for was four trees to my right.

'Vali, is that you?' she asked.

'No Nani, it's me, Tanaaz,' I replied.

'Oh Tanaaz, you are here. Come give me a hug,' she said.

I suppose you should never argue with your grandmother, especially if she is wielding a weapon.

'Come, carry this.' She handed me a quiver full of arrows.

I hung on to the quiver, warily wondering how sharp the tips might be.

‘Did you have a safe trip?’ she asked.

‘Yes Nani,’ I mumbled.

‘What are you doing running around like that in the orchard?’ she asked.

‘Just trying to catch up with Wasif,’ I said.

‘You better find him and come inside, both of you, before it gets too dark,’ she said, looking around. ‘Sunset is at five, you know.’

Right, everything was different here.

‘A true winter. Something you Bombay-ites might enjoy, don’t you think?’ she smiled. ‘We can light up the old fireplace in your room.’

We both looked at each other, and then our collective memory flickered to a certain incident. Nani had grabbed a thin wooden log thinking it was the iron stoker. Dad had seen the leaping flames and jumped into action. He’d caught hold of the log and managed to quickly shove it back into the fireplace, but not before there was black soot everywhere. Soot that we had to clean.

‘Ya, no,’ we said at the same time.

I guess her vision hasn't really gotten better since then. 'Heaters are much safer then,' she said, walking briskly ahead.

'Cleaner too,' I agreed.

At least I managed to beat Wasif back home. Dinner was a glum affair, though Wasif and I were busy in a desi scarf-off seeing who could down the most parathas. Not really a bad competition given Sharfu Chacha's parathas were gleaming with homemade white butter. Vali was still chewing the one paratha his mom had put on his plate. He had his book propped under the table and moved his mouth when he turned a page. Sehar was sneaking messages on her phone and ignoring Urooj, who was done with her meal. She too was peering at her phone and building a jenga-like tower made up of what look like mini magnetic tiles.

The only one making circles around the dining table was Wasif's baby sister Xenia, followed by her mother Rukhsana Mammi. 'Xenia, I am not going to run after you!' she said as she ran after her, trying to feed her.

'Miaow miaow,' she said, petting the yo-yo that she was vigorously pulling along.

'Kitty cat?' she said, picking up the yo-yo for Nana to pet.

'Ho ho,' Nana bellowed, holding Xenia on his lap and petting the yo-yo. 'This is the only pet I will allow in the house. And this is a good time to remind everyone of the other rules.'

Nana, who had a long career in the military, had a few rules we always had to follow. He listed them to us as if our parents ever let us forget:

1. BE HOME BEFORE DARK.
2. NO ROAMING AROUND THE HOUSE AFTER DARK.
3. TWO GLASSES OF MILK EVERY DAY.
4. EAT YOUR SERVING OF MAKHANA, BADAAM AND WALNUTS EVERY DAY.
5. NO EATING ANY STREET FOOD.
6. BE UP EARLY. (EVEN ON HOLIDAYS)
7. NO PETS ALLOWED.
8. SPEAK LOUDLY (THIS WAS MAINLY BECAUSE HE WAS HARD OF HEARING).

No sleeping in, no excursions for chaat. What a boring two weeks this was going to be.

Suddenly the lights went out. **BANG! CRASH!** We heard a clatter of dishes in the kitchen. 'Candles, candles, get the candles,' said Nani, springing up. Sehar switched on her phone's flashlight and went to help Ammi rummage for candles in the sideboard.

Thuut, thuut, thutt.

A persistent tapping on the window had Urooj jump out of her chair. 'W . . . whhhat was that?' she stuttered.

'Just the trees tapping on the window, beta, nothing to be scared of,' Qamar Khala said.

I took this as my cue to head to the window. Wasif joined in; at least we both had the same idea.

'I swear I left my glasses on the table upstairs,' said Dad. 'How are they here?'

'Oh, that must be the jinn,' said Sharfu Chacha off-handedly, as he began clearing the table.

'Jinn?' Sehar gulped.

'Hain, always misplacing things here and there. Yesterday

I found my karchi in the upar wala kamra,' he explained, dramatically moving his hands so that elongated shadows danced on the wall.

'Mirchi? Yes, there was a little bit too much mirchi in the dal today,' said Nana, nodding his head.

Meanwhile, Wasif and I crept behind Sehar and Urooj, who were huddled together on the sofa with Ammi and Qamar Khala, and lodged ourselves in the curtains.

'Ohhh, aahhh,' we howled, moving our hands in an exaggerated manner.

'Ammi, please tell them to stop, it's not funny!' said Sehar.

'What, a little power outage and the dark night scaring you off?' I chided.

'No, but your ghost sounds like he has a sore throat!' said Urooj. She and Urooj started giggling. I guess some of the ice was beginning to thaw.

Sharfu Chacha cleared up the table and said he was retiring to his room.

'Bachalog ka samaan upar wale kamra mein rakh diya hoon', he said.

I looked woefully at Wasif. 'Are we all in the same room?'

'Yup, same as last time,' he said.

He led us up the stairs and past the landing on the first floor where Nana, Nani and our parents were put up in their respective rooms. Sehar and Urooj were holding hands as we walked up the second flight of stairs. Our shadows had a growth spurt in the candlelight creeping along on the wall opposite the staircase.

'Boo!' shouted Xenia from the door of her bedroom on the first floor, just as Sharfu Chacha opened the door to our room with an ominous screech.

'Ahhhhh!' we all screamed.

Sharfu Chacha pointed out the heater and the light switches for when the lights would be back. He left the candle in the now defunct fireplace. The flame cast shadows all around the room. Black soot coated the fireplace and you could see a telling black line all the way to the ceiling. Cots were lined up military style, with Nani's trademark scratchy woollen blankets laid on top in what looked like army-issued battalion green. The room, and the night, looked as dreary as we felt.

BOO!

CHAPTER 3

December 17: Target Practice

I could hear some scratching and rustling sounds at the edge of my sleep. I tossed and turned to drown them out. They calmed for a bit and then began in full force a few moments later. Thinking it was Vali cranking up the heater, I told him to pipe down.

'It's not me,' he squeaked back.

Then it had to be Wasif trying to prank me.

'Wasif, cut it out!' I yelled. I opened my eyes, irritated, and rose up to see him.

'Not me,' he whispered.

Wasif was looking straight up at the ceiling with the blanket drawn all the way to his face. He looked terrified. Urooj was fast asleep, Sehar was snoring softly. So it couldn't be them. Vali, Wasif, and I all looked up to the ceiling and on cue the rustling and scratching picked up again!

'Arrgh!' we screamed, grabbed our blankets and ran downstairs.

I woke up being poked by a stick. 'Why are you here on the sofa when there is a perfectly serviceable bed for you?' asked the towering, blurry frame of Nana, as my eyes regained their focus.

He must have woken up early and seen the three of us bunched together in front of the fireplace.

'There are sounds coming from the attic!' Vali said. 'Strange, shuffling, scratching and rustling noises. It sounded like mice!'

'Lice—don't be silly, they barely make a sound,' he waved his hand dismissively. 'Sharfu, take a look.'

'Take a look at what, Baba?' asked Rasheed Mammu, entering the room and pulling out a monkey cap from the basket by the fireplace.

'The attic. Lice they say . . . more likely some busy mice. These brave children had to spend the night in the living room,' Nana said, pointing to our bedraggled sleeping arrangement.

'I'll take a look,' said Rasheed Mammu, bounding up the stairs two steps at a time.

As we settled down for a breakfast of malida, mushroom omelettes, buttered toast and warm milk, Ammi asked if we slept at all. 'You look so tired.'

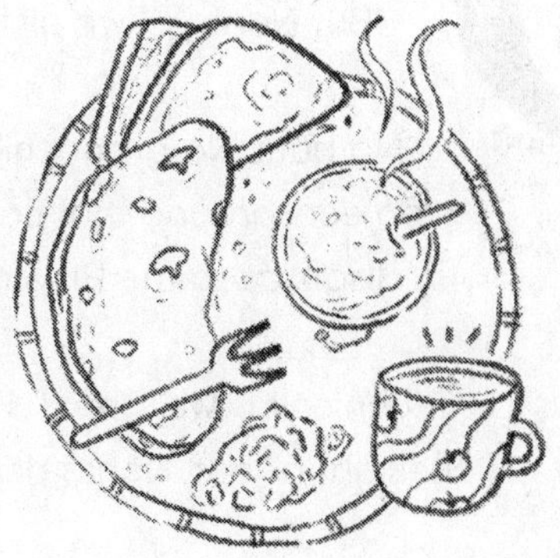

'There were strange noises coming from the attic, Parveen Phuphu,' whispered Vali.

‘Oh that! Old houses creak all the time. Clearly your sisters didn’t have any problems,’ Ammi said, pointing to Sehar and Urooj.

‘Noises? What noises?’ asked Sehar.

‘Didn’t you hear them? Rustling, shuffling, scratching,’ said Wasif.

‘Couldn’t hear a thing over Sehar’s snoring.’

This earned Urooj an ill-timed piece of toast over her head.

‘Tut, tut, Sehar, you must aim better. You kids are getting too soft. Don’t your parents teach you anything these days?’ asked Nani. ‘Target practice near the cabin in twenty minutes.’

‘But Nani . . . ’ we all began all together.

‘No buts. No grandchildren of mine are going to throw objects around that can’t even hit their intended target. A disgrace to the Rizvi name.’

‘Technically, we aren’t Rizvis,’ I pointed out, but failing eyesight or not, Nani’s death glare was still intact.

As soon as breakfast was over, the six of us, bundled up in sweaters, mufflers and monkey caps, were led out by Nani. Nani's cropped silver hair shone in the gold dusting of the sun. She cut a striking figure in her blue woollen shalwar kameez topped by a colourful pheran. She was holding Xenia, who was making woofing sounds over a stick that she'd convinced Nani to tie a string around. The stick bounced off Nani's back as Xenia looked over her shoulder to grin at the rest of us.

'I can't get CPR and now this,' Sehar said, poking me.

'Hello, it was your poor aim that inspired her!' I pointed out.

'Why do you need cardiopulmonary resuscitation?' asked Vali, looking confused.

'Cell phone reception, Vali,' huffed Sehar.

'Silly billies scared of some noises!' Urooj puffed, linking her hand in the crook of Sehar's arm as they walked ahead of us. What? Now both Sehar and Urooj were ganging up against us!

The cabin was a short walk from the house. It was a small squat wooden building made up entirely of wood. There was a wooden door with a latch that led into a small room, which looked like a pine tree had thrown up. There was wood on the ceiling, on the walls, on the floor. Everything in

the cabin was a boring shade of brown.

On the walls were a few hooks that held quivers of arrows. A number of differently shaped bows leaned against the wall. Nani's practice equipment. Her prized bow with which she had won numerous local and national competitions was kept under lock and key in a cabinet in the study. We all trudged towards the bows.

'And where do you think you are going?' enquired Nani.

We stopped mid-step and turned around. 'To get the bows?' Wasif said.

'And what makes you think I would trust you with my bows?' asked Nani with one eyebrow raised like an arch-villain. 'Take these arrows outside.' She pointed to a basket with a bunch of arrows near a wall.

We walked to a tree in the middle of the orchard, which had a target painted at the centre—a red circle, ensconced by a white one and finally a big blue circle.

'OK line up. You are going to try to make a bullseye,' said Nani.

'With just arrows?' Vali asked. He was a stickler for doing things the way they were meant to be done.

'Sure, before you move on to bows,' explained Nani. 'Xenia beta, stay here with me, let's see how your cousins shoot.'

We lined up from the tallest to the smallest and aimed the arrows at the target. While we mainly hit at the white and blue spots on the target, the arrows bounced off the tree and landed helter-skelter, a few feet away.

A crisscrossing mass of arrows lined the orchard floor, much to Nani's dismay. She lectured us on the correct stance and showed us how to close one eye, keep the target in focus and throw with just the right amount of force. As the experienced practitioner of the sport steadied her arm and let off a flying arrow, it landed two trees away.

We all looked at her in shock. 'Ah, well, my eyesight isn't what it used to be. I guess it's target practice for us all then,' she said.

CHAPTER 4

December 18: Time Slows Down

A funny thing happens when we are at Nana-Nani's house. Time always slows down. Other than our bouts of (mandatory) target practice, we had the whole day (and night) to ourselves. The very next day, we were marched to the orchard for our mandatory target practice and returned by mid-morning to join everyone basking in the sun on the terrace upstairs.

It was a humongous terrace from where we could see the steepled roof with its slate-shingle tile and a rather magnificent view of the Himalayas with their snow-covered peaks. Everyone grabbed their spot in the sun, to lounge on chairs and charpoys. While Nana took his hookah and read the papers, everyone else gathered for chai and Rukhsana

Mammi's delicious collection of biscuits and big, heaped servings of boiled peanuts.

As the adults cracked and popped open the peanuts, the heap of peanut shells on the thali grew bigger and bigger. I grabbed a handful, leaned over the railing and shucked them at the moving target of Sharfu Chacha in the garden path downstairs. He would look up now and again to see what had hit him and I would quickly duck and laugh.

'Amateur move,' said Wasif. 'He can easily guess it's you.'

'Okay Peanut Pro, what's your idea?'

He smiled slyly and pointed to the bamboo ladder in the corner of the terrace that led to a small parapet. I had to admit that the raised siding of the parapet meant that we had good cover.

Wasif quietly picked up the thali that held all the peanut shells and we walked to the ladder. I climbed up first, while he followed with the thali. We now had a bird's eye view of the terrace, Sharfu Chacha downstairs and the attic window right above us.

I giggled and grabbed a bunch of peanut shells to rain down on the others. We aimed at Qaisar Khalu and Omair

Mammu who moved ever so slightly while snoring. No peanut shells were going to interrupt their siesta. Dad was engrossed in his newspaper and a shower of peanut shells did nothing to bother him. Rasheed Mammu was on the phone, deep in conversation, glancing occasionally at the attic window. We managed to get one peanut shell to land on his monkey cap but it promptly got stuck in the red pompom.

Another handful of shells made their way to Urooj's collection of magnetic tiles, cubes, balls and other things that stick. Sehar and Urooj had long forgotten their co-ord set war and were building some sort of elaborate ramp. Xenia was testing the ramp with her collection of 'pets'—an acorn, some peanuts, and her hand-sewn menagerie of wild animals.

The adults were taking turns with the newspaper and other assorted books and magazines from Nana and Nani's still-growing collection. 'No one reads these days,' Nana would mutter occasionally, earning a sympathetic glance from Ammi and an offended look from Vali.

'I read,' he said, 'all the time.'

JINN!
ZZZ
Z

Rukhsana Mammi and Qamar Khala were engaged in a contentious game of carrom. Even our precision aim at their shawl-draped heads didn't distract them. They were down to the fight for the queen. 'Ab dekhen oont kis karwat baithata hai,' said Qamar Khala, rubbing her hands.

'Why would a camel eat bitter gourd?' asked Urooj.

'Uff, not karela, karwat—to turn,' explained Qamar Khala.

Rukhsana Mammi looked like she had cornered the queen. 'I'll eat a plate of karela if I can't make this shot!'

Just as she aimed and let go of the striker with a thwack, Wasif's elbow nudged the thali of peanut shells, which toppled over the parapet ledge and right onto Sharfu Chacha's cushiony head.

Jinn! Jinn!'

'Bas, Bibiji, I am leaving!'

CHAPTER 5

December 19: Snug as a Bug in a . . .

'Rise and shine, sleepy-heads!' said Rasheed Mammu, poking his head into our room.

'What time is it?' I asked.

'8 a.m.,' said Urooj.

'No self-respecting kid on holiday gets up at 8 a.m., Mammu.' I pulled the blanket over my head.

'Actually, early morning sunlight helps regulate circadian rhythm and boosts production of vitamin D. Also, you can improve cognition and focus. And even sleep better at night,' Vali informed us.

I did my best to glare at Vali. Easy for him to say. Vali's noise-cancelling headphones were on his bed while Wasif and I had to stuff our ears with cotton. At least the scratching and rustling sounds were now muffled, like they came from far away. If we couldn't hear the jinn, we couldn't do its bidding now, could we?

I turned around to see Vali all dressed up and it may have been the sun's early morning rays but I swear his glasses looked like they had been polished up to a shine. Wasif threw a pillow in his general direction, which landed on Rasheed Mammu, who lost his grip on the knotted plastic bag he'd been holding, causing it to fall.

'Ew what's that smell?' asked Sehar, wrinkling up her nose.

'Oh nothing, just cleaning up the attic,' he said quickly, shoving little pellets and tissues back into the bag. 'Make them hurry up, Vali. The museum isn't open all day,' he said as he ran out of the room.

Urooj mumbled, 'Dwiis he sai musom?'

Wasif took out the cotton out of his ears. 'What?'

She yawned and said again, 'Did he say museum?'

'Yes,' said Vali, excitedly pulling out his laptop and opening up the City Museum website. He read, 'The Solan City Museum houses a collection of taxidermy specimens of the local fauna as well as a lively history of Solan—past and present—from a colonial hill station to an ecological example of sustainability and progress.'

'Who plans boring museum trips on a vacation?' groaned Sehar.

'We aren't even awake yet!' complained Wasif.

'You had better be soon—Nana will be doing roll call,' warned Vali, followed by a poor imitation of Nana's 'Hurry! Hurry! Jaldi! Jaldi!'.

Only Vali said 'Jaaldee, Jaaldee', which sounded like an angry English general threatening his rebellious army. Except, we weren't particularly rebellious, just mostly inert.

'What is this, a military camp? Why aren't we even allowed to sleep in?' said Urooj. 'Besides, aren't they worried the heirs to the Rizvi name aren't getting their beauty sleep?'

'Tell that to Nana, who wants to give us all an education in our roots,' I sighed.

'I'd rather have wings and fly away,' Sehar said as she turned over.

'We could make a detour to get some kheema patties and cream puffs from Morrison's,' I suggested.

'Oh, what are those? I don't think Ammi will let us,' said Urooj intrigued.

'And who's going to tell her?' said Wasif.

'It will be rather hard not to, if she is, you know, right there,' Urooj reasoned.

'We just have to come up with a plan,' I said, excited to finally have a purpose.

'SEHAR! TANAAZ! UROOJ! WASIF!' came Nana's bellowing voice, which had the intended effect of speeding up the Rizvi (and not Rizvi) cousins!

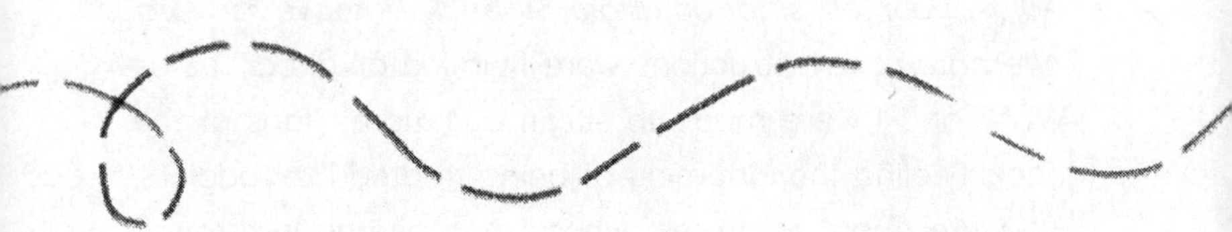

'We are all going in that?' asked Urooj in a doubtful voice. 'Isn't that umm . . . against the law or something?'

'Not against the laws of Indian families and the art of stuffing an Ambassador car,' replied Rasheed Mammu. The red pompom on his monkey cap bobbed up and down as he rubbed his hands gleefully. 'I learned to drive on this beauty the same year I trained with Suresh at the Forest Department,' he said, which, if you did the math, meant the car had been around for a long, long time.

Xenia, dressed in her unicorn sweater and pink-and-purple sunglasses, didn't need to be told twice. She climbed onto the ledge at the back and called it her beach chair. Ammi, Qamar Khala and Rukhsana Mammi got into the back, beckoning Sehar to sit beside them. Dad sat next to Rasheed Mammu, while Qaisar Khalu shimmied in next to him. Vali sat on his lap, precariously protruding out the window.

Adjust yourself, sit at an angle. Sit back, I'll move forward. Alternate now. Instructions were flying in all directions as Wasif and I were made to sit on our moms' laps at the back. Feeling the ignominy of being treated like toddlers, we were about to protest when Nana peered in through the windows.

‘All set?’ he asked. More like all stuffed! Thankfully Nana, Nani and Omair Mammu were staying home.

‘Don’t forget to see the Hall of Change exhibit and take pictures,’ Nana advised.

‘Is there going to be a quiz?’ asked Vali excitedly.

With a lurch and shudder, the car started and Rasheed Mammu drove it in an arc, leading it away from Naz Manzil and down the hill towards the main town. I waved at Nana and Nani, who were standing at the doorway and looking up at the attic window. Probably Omair Mammu up there.

With a few bumps and loud conversations, we arrived at the Solan City Museum, an old Victorian mansion with a bank of windows gleaming in the sunshine. We all tumbled out of the Ambassador, a jumble of cramped limbs and squished bottoms, into the crisp, pine-scented winter air. The visitors at the museum were considerably sparse. No surprise, since it was a sunshiny day and no sensible person (aka not the Rizvi family) would want to waste it being indoors.

Vali was practically vibrating with excitement. The two-storey mansion was chock-a-block with things from before our time. The parents and kids split up, agreeing to meet at the bottom of the palatial staircase in an hour's time. Ammi (a school teacher) and Vali (an eager student) decided to explore the top floor while the rest of us chose to start downstairs. We walked through room after room filled with ancient coins, paintings, sculptures and handicrafts.

In one of the rooms, was a large hand loom with an elderly lady weaving thread and creating a local handloom design. Urooj peppered her with questions (translated via Qamar Khala and Qaisar Khalu) about the kind of wool, the designs, and the traditional patterns she was using. Her eyes shone as she watched the lady working the loom with deft hands.

Sehar was just excited to get out of the house and kept looking for a signal so she could call her friends to fuel her FOMO. Wasif and I spotted a long corridor. He looked at me and raised three fingers. With a 3 . . . 2 . . . 1 . . . we both ran, speeding past blurred images of animals and birds.

Dang it! Wasif was in the lead again! I turned the corner when I heard a sharp yelp. Wasif was face to face, rather, face to nose with a towering six-foot stuffed yak.

'It belongs to the Bovini tribe. So, cousins with bison, buffaloes and cattle,' said a small voice behind us. Wasif and I both jumped.

Vali kept reading off a plaque by the base of the creature. 'It can tolerate temperatures as low as minus forty degrees Celsius. Adapted to living at high altitudes, yaks have long hair that hangs off their sides like a curtain, sometimes touching the ground. They are highly valued by the Himalayan people. According to a Tibetan legend, the first yaks were domesticated by the Tibetans.' He looked up and beamed.

'Thanks, braini-yak,' I said and we all burst out laughing. Hmm. If they were laughing at my jokes, maybe spending time with family wasn't all that bad.

Our squeals of laughter probably alerted the others, because they all spilled into the room.

We examined the other taxidermy exhibits—there was

a life-size stuffed black bear, pheasants and musk deer. Urooj kept trying to stroke the yak's long hair. 'Can we get some yak wool, please?' she begged Qamar Khala.

Sehar took selfies with the animals and was currently posing with a snow leopard. Qamar Khala pointed to a brightly coloured pheasant bird. 'That's the monal,' she said. 'When we were growing up, we used to see them around all the time.'

Qaisar Khalu, Dad and Rasheed Mammu were huddled around a small exhibit in a glass case. We pushed in closer and stuck our noses to the glass. 'Bat cave!' yelled Wasif.

'Fruit bats in India face shrinking forests. And the lack of food sources means they have to fly thousands of kilometres in a day. This makes them efficient pollinators, carrying seed and other pollen on their furry bodies. Flying foxes can carry pollen for up to 100 km in one night,' read Vali. 'Flying foxes are fast eaters and can digest their food in fifteen to twenty minutes. While flying they can drop around 60,000 seeds along the way!'

'Cool!' Wasif, Vali and I said together while at the exact same time Sehar and Urooj exclaimed, 'Gross!'

While Wasif and I did our best Batman impersonations to an unimpressed stuffed bat audience, Ammi poked her head into the room. Her smile was bright and her long silver earring dangled in excitement. 'Come on, come on, you have to see if there is someone you know in these hallowed halls.'

'Unfortunately, we not only know them but we are also related to these monkeys,' said Urooj, pointing to us. She and Sehar both laughed as they followed Ammi out of the room. It sounded like Sehar was also having a good time.

We followed behind them, trooping up the large staircase in the middle of the entrance lobby.

'What exactly are we looking for?' asked Wasif.

'No idea,' I replied.

'Was this the quiz Nana was talking about?' asked Vali hopefully.

We walked into a room full of trophies, medals and medallions hanging on the wall. There were old pictures of men in smart military uniforms accepting medals and mountaineers affixing the Indian flag on high Himalayan peaks. There was also a collection of swords and crests dotting the walls. Qamar Khala beckoned us to a black-

and-white portrait of a man dressed in a stuffy suit and tie, handing a huge trophy to a sharp-nosed, short-haired lady dressed in a sari. She was holding her trophy with her long, dainty, bejewelled fingers and an unmistakable smile.

'Nani!' we yelled in unison.

The plaque read: 'Mrs Nazneen Rizvi receives the National Archery Award from His Excellency the Honourable Shri Gautam Kumar Virk at the All-Women's Archery Tournament, 1954. Solan Residency Club, Solan.'

Sehar stage-directed us as we tried different permutations and combinations to fit the whole family in a selfie with our world-famous, at least India-famous . . . okay Solan-famous Nani!

CHAPTER 6

December 20: Midnight Feast

'I am hungry,' I sighed.

'Me too,' said Wasif.

'Me three,' agreed Vali.

'Me four,' came another voice—Urooj.

'Me five,' said Sehar.

This was another first. All five of us in agreement about something. I suspect our running around in the orchard in the evening had something to do with it.

'Let's go downstairs. I know Ammi's brought a whole carton of Kurkure,' said Sehar, brushing aside her blanket.

'Don't you dare. You'll overeat, get an upset stomach and keep the rest of us awake all night,' I warned.

'It's not like you aren't awake half the night anyhow, staring at the ceiling,' she shot back.

Just then, we heard it again. The scratching and the rustling. We all looked up.

What could it be? Sharfu Chacha said it was jinn. Maybe it was just a lost cat? Our mammus kept taking turns to go up there to check, but we still had no answers.

'OK well, still hungry,' said Wasif.

'Vali and Tanaaz, go check if all the adults are asleep,' commanded Sehar. 'I will go down first and the rest can follow me.'

'And why do you get to be the first one down?' I asked, annoyed.

Sehar lifted her phone, which is physically attached to her arm at all times, and pointed the flashlight directly at the rest of us.

Vali and I quickly went on our recon mission and reported back that all the adults (plus Xenia) were likely sleeping since there were no lights or sound anywhere. Sehar walked ahead confidently, pointing the flashlight on the staircase.

'Quietly,' she said. All of us tiptoed down the stairs.

Creaaaakk, went the noisy stairs as we started walking down.

'Shh!' said Sehar, turning to Urooj and putting a finger to her lips.

'Shh!' Urooj turned to Wasif and lightly slapped his head.

'Shhh!' said Wasif, pinching Vali's hand, and—

'Shhhh!' Vali said to me as if I couldn't hear all the shushing.

Holding on to each other's sweaters, we figured out the way to the kitchen in the dark. The old wooden floors squeaked in protest as if to admonish us back to bed.

'Don't bump into the sideboard,' whispered Sehar.

Finally in the kitchen, she switched on the light at the same time as we heard the beeping of the microwave. And then an audible gasp.

Ammi, Qamar Khala and Rukhsana Mammi were in the kitchen! Ammi was by the microwave while Qamar Khala and Rukhsana Mammi were standing next to the nematkhana, Nani's little pantry cupboard that she still used to store food despite having a fridge. Bundled up in shawls, and what looked like Nana's dressing gown, our mothers looked back and forth at each other and then at us.

'Just er . . . came down to get some hot water,' Rukhsana Mammi stammered, pointing to a steaming pot on the stove.

'Yes, so cold—hamari toh kulfi jum gayi,' Qamar Khala agreed.

'If it's so cold, why are you freezing kulfi?' Vali asked, looking puzzled.

'Uff, we are frozen like . . . ' began Qamar Khala, when Sehar interrupted. ‘Wait, why does it smell like gur?’ she asked.

‘Oh, you know, gur warms the body,’ said Ammi in her most teacher-like voice.

‘But I don’t think you will like it,’ added Rukhsana Mammi quickly.

‘It smells nice,’ said Vali.

‘Can we try some?’ asked Wasif.

‘What are you doing here in the middle of the night anyway?’ whispered Qamar Khala.

‘We could ask you the same question,’ replied Urooj.

‘We were ...er...’ she started.

‘So are we,’ Urooj finished the sentence.

The microwave beeped indignantly again, annoyed at being ignored. Ammi opened the microwave and a waft of sweet cardamom-scented chai filled the room. ‘Chai in the microwave? Sharfu Chacha won’t approve,’ said Sehar, crossing her arms.

‘Who is going to tell . . . I mean . . . it’s instant . . . ’ started Qamar Khala when the hot water on the stovetop hissed and let out steam.

'Oh, it's done,' said Rukhsana Mammi, grabbing a towel and turning off the stove in one swift motion.

Our moms and aunts looked at each other and sighed.

'I guess there's no point in taking food away from growing kids,' reasoned Qamar Khala.

'But they are taking it away from us!' cried Rukhsana Mammi.

'Come on, all of you. No use trying to have a midnight feast by ourselves,' said Ammi.

We gathered around the kitchen table as Rukhsana Mammi placed the huge steaming pot on the table. Ammi and Qamar Khala grabbed some plates and spoons. As they clattered, everyone shushed everyone else.

'Be quiet or you'll wake up the others,' warned Qamar Khala.

'Better not, there isn't enough for everyone,' said Ammi practically.

Rukhsana Mammi carefully took off the lid of the steamer and we saw two plump crescent-shaped buns. 'Siddu!' we

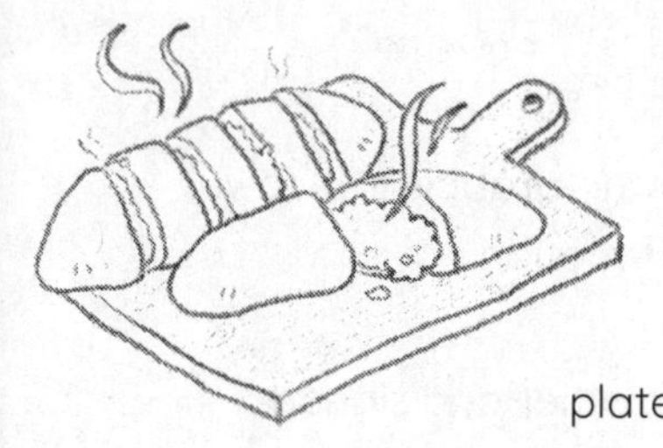

all cried out. Nani used to make platters of these delicious stuffed buns every time we visited. Ammi took out the siddus and carefully sliced them, while Qamar Khala plated them and passed them around.

'I know what would go well with this!' Sehar rushed to the nematkhanna and took out the spottiest bananas that were one black spot short of rotting. 'Quick, line up some mugs,' said Sehar and very soon everyone was following her directions:

Mugs!
Baking powder!
Peanut butter! (Ya, no. Yuck!)
Cacao powder!

We mixed the ingredients, placed a square of Dairy Milk chocolate in the centre and lined up the mugs for their one-minute transformations into (hopefully edible) mug cakes. 'Trust me, it's a viral recipe,' said Sehar.

MUSICAL MASALA

One minute later, the microwave beeped and we stared at a gooey mass of, um, something.
'Go on, try it,' Sehar nudged me to take the first bite.

'Hot hot hot!' I whisper-screamed.

A more cautious Wasif tried a little bit less with his spoon. 'Yum!' he said.

Soon, the rest of us were polishing off our individual mug cakes. We mixed and matched siddu drizzled with ghee and warm chocolate mug cakes. All in all, it was a warm, gooey, memorable mess of a midnight feast!

CHAPTER 7

December 21: Ice Cold

The laws of winter dictate that you eat more, and move less. You lie snug in warm blankets but can feel how cold the air is because the tip of your nose is stone cold. You know it is daytime, but it feels like night.

Or maybe that's because Urooj was blocking the one window that let in some light.

'Fifteen, sixteen, seventeen . . . '

'What are you doing?' I asked.

'Why can't I get any sleep around here?' complained Sehar.

'Eighteen. Sharfu Chacha says if you see a dozen or more snowflakes it means, get ready for a snowstorm!' Urooj clapped her hands in glee.

We all gathered at the lone window to see flurries of snow flying softly. I had never seen snow before. It looked like whispers of white feathers falling gently through the air.

The barren trees caught the snow in their branches. Some snowflakes fell softly to the ground. All around us, the houses and rooftops were blanketed in a soft white glow.

Wheee . . . Bang! Clank!

We all looked up at the ceiling, but this time the noise had come from somewhere else. Wasif stepped out of the bathroom onto the landing with a puzzled look on his face.

'Did the toilet make strange bubbling noises when you flushed it?' he asked.

Bang! Clank! Whee . . .

We all walked to the bathroom door and gingerly opened it to hear strange gurgling and whistling noises.

'The jinn!' I screamed.

'Bhoot! Jinn!' yelled Wasif.

'Boohoo-jii!' Vali cried.

Clearly the jinn or bhoot was becoming bolder and bolder and didn't want to stay confined to the attic. Nani had always told us that jinn usually lived in the bathroom. Now they were coming for us! We all ran downstairs.

'What are you all yelling about?' asked Rukhsana Mammi, quickly swallowing the last remnants of some khari.

'The Bhoot-Jinn is making strange sounds in the bathroom,' panted Urooj.

'Oh,' she said, suddenly serious. 'Whistling?'

'Yes,' we nodded.

'Gurgling?'

'Yes, yes,' we shook our heads.

'Bubbles in the toilet?'

'Yes! Yes! Yes!'

'SHARFU CHACHA!' Rukhsana Mammi screamed, startling us all. 'The pipes are frozen again.'

Sharfu Chacha appeared with a little tin can filled with wood chips. 'I know, I know. I just got some water going in the kitchen sink. I'll take a look upstairs,' he muttered, making a slow ascent. Curious, we followed him up.

'Frozen solid,' he said as he opened all the faucets. The

water, barely a trickle before, had stopped all together now. 'Uff,' he said as he sat on his haunches and placed the tin can directly under the tap. He took out a matchbox, lit a match and threw it into the tin can!

Fire! In the bathroom! This day was getting better. He grinned as he looked at our astonished faces. 'Oh, you plains-people, don't you know anything? To melt the water in the pipes. Heat it up, little by little,' he explained, shaking his head.

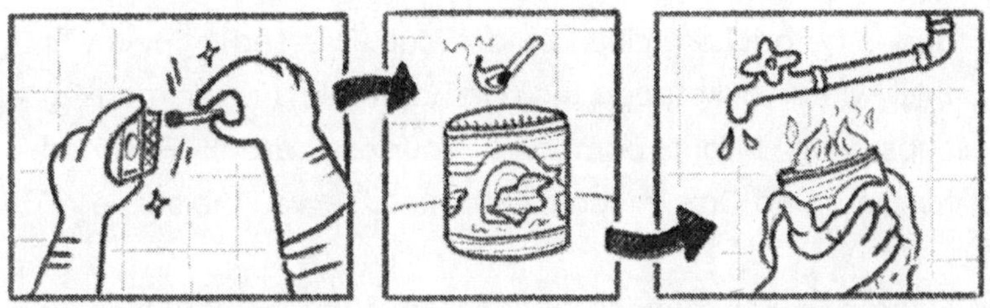

On cue, some water came trickling down and he quickly placed the ancient steel bucket underneath to catch the dribble. Three more bathrooms to go. 'Can we try?' I asked eagerly. He slapped my hand away and told me to go downstairs and bring up some more wood chips from the kitchen. Wasif, Vali and I ran up and down, following Sharfu Chacha's instructions. He showed us how to position the tin can, carefully light a match and place the warm leaping flames directly under the taps to loosen up the ice and get something to come out of the taps.

Once he realized that the water was still barely a trickle, he cocked his head to the side, and said, 'Let's go.' We followed him downstairs, and out into the covered patio. He opened a storage cupboard and instructed us to gather a bunch of buckets, small shovels and spades. Then we marched out into the icy cold backyard.

Sharfu Chacha started a wood fire with a huge patila close to the covered patio. We gathered snow in buckets, and dumped it into the pot. He stoked the fire and we watched fascinated as the snow melted.

Soon, the adults trickled outside too. Dressed in layers of thick winter jackets courtesy Qamar Khala and tan monkey caps with bright pompoms courtesy Urooj, Rasheed Mammu and Omair Mammu came to survey the scene.

Nana and Xenia joined us too, with Nana mostly chasing Xenia, who was running around in her snowsuit. Nana, whose jacket was covered in shark stickers, kept trying to tell her to stay in one place. He careened her off to the side, where they built a giant snowman. Urooj ran in to grab a scarf for the snowman, while Sehar gathered sticks for his arms. We found acorns for his eyes and nose and little used-up lumps of firewood for his lopsided smile. Xenia kept trying to tie a string onto the snowman and lead him into the house.

Just as Omair Mammu turned to head indoors, thwack! A snowball hit him square in the back, showering powdered snow all over. 'Oh no you didn't!' he yelled at Rasheed Mammu, who was in a fit of giggles. Taking his cue, we gathered the freshly fallen snow into compact little snowballs and launched them! I got Wasif on his neck. In response, I got a snowball on my shoulder.

Urooj and Sehar ganged up with Rasheed Mammu while Omair Mammu took us under his wing. He showed us how to compact the snow to create a snowball with maximum density. We ducked and hid behind the old Ambassador, which was now just a big lump of snow. Even Vali got a few hits bang on Rasheed Mammu's neck!

After that, it was a free-for-all. Snowballs were flying, our fingers were numb from the cold and squeals of delight echoed through the orchard. At least, for once, target practice was paying off!

CHAPTER 8

December 22: A Sticky Situation

'Big it,' said Xenia, handing me a bright blue balloon.

I dutifully filled my lungs and exhaled all the air into the balloon, knotted it and handed it over.

She grinned and moved on to Wasif. 'Big it,' she commanded, handing him another blue balloon.

It was a rather gloomy day. The skies were grey and the cold had us all huddled indoors in the living room around the roaring fireplace. Sehar and Urooj were whispering about something, as Urooj built a complicated tower with her magnetic tiles and Sehar strung some magnetic beads into a necklace.

Vali and Ammi were as usual curled up in a corner reading, surrounded by a book fort. Nani was dozing off by the fire, while Qaisar Khalu, Qamar Khala and Rukhsana Mammi were engrossed in a card game. From the corridor we could hear Xenia accosting Nana in his study with the stern command to 'big it'.

The smell of frying onions came wafting into the room so my tummy naturally led the way to the kitchen. I opened the door to see Dad pottering about the kitchen, shouting instructions to Omair Mammu and Rasheed Mammu.

'Tanaaz, good, come here. Shell these peas,' he said.

Me? I didn't remember volunteering to actually do anything. I mean, other than eat.

Sharfu Chacha looked aghast. 'Who puts peas in haleem?'

'It's green,' reasoned Dad. 'We need something green.'

'So add green chillies,' Chacha huffed, as he walked over to the kitchen sink to wash, by my count, at least four different kinds of lentils.

Rasheed Mammu was frying the onions while Omair Mammu kept looking in the back of the storeroom for apples. 'I swear I put a box full of ripe ones here,' he muttered.

'Apples?' called Sharfu Chacha, draining the water from the red lentils, as any remaining colour drained from his face. 'Parvez miyan, you can't possibly want to put apples in haleem.'

I didn't think apples in haleem was a good idea either.

'No, no the box had some worms for the b . . .' said Omair Mammu, stopping short.

Rasheed Mammu gave Omair Mammu a quick rap with the jhara.

'Ow! Umm . . . er . . . for the compost pit,' he said, nursing his knuckles.

'Outside, I put them outside,' said a relieved Sharfu Chacha.

Omair Mammu put on his monkey cap with the orange bobbing pompom and stepped outside.

I was trying to keep track of the peas but more often than not, some errant peas would pop out of their pod with force and scatter over the kitchen floor.

'Careful, we do want to have some to eat as well, not sacrificed to the floor,' chided Dad. A cold draft and the smell of overripe apples engulfed the kitchen as Omair Mammu hurried in, and out of the kitchen.

'Peeled, fried and washed,' said Wasif, materializing out of nowhere, using martial arts moves to point to said peeled peas, fried onions and washed dals.

'Excellent,' said Dad rubbing his hands on a dishcloth and examining the contents of our labour. Wasif's karate moves meant only one thing—he was gearing up for battle, which meant I had to be ready to bolt. I mean, to fight back.

Except, there was a huge, heavy degh in my way. Sharfu Chacha had yanked it from its perch under the counter and was dislodging the other deghs that lay nestled inside like a desi version of a Matryoshka doll.

'Sharfu Chacha, pressure cooker, please,' said Dad. Sharfu Chacha stopped mid-degh-dislodging to glare at Dad.

'You can't possibly be thinking of cooking haleem in a pressure cooker,' he scoffed.

'It will be quick quick quick,' said Dad, moving all the dals into one big bowl. 'I don't suppose you have an InstaPot?'

Sharfu Chacha left the big and baby deghs stranded on the kitchen floor and pointed to the offending pressure cooker on the kitchen counter. Shaking his head, he moved towards the kitchen door mumbling, 'Never thought I would live to see the day . . . slow burning wood fire . . . cooked overnight haleem . . . pressure cooker . . . insta what? It's an insult is what it is . . . Insta haleem . . .
Bibiji, I am . . .'

I made full use of this distraction to lob past Wasif and pushed him into the strewn deghs. I was off before I heard him land with a loud crash and raced upstairs to the bedroom. Despite my considerable lead, I could hear him moving up the stairs two at a time, vowing to reintroduce his fists to my face. I had almost shut the door when he burst in.

That's when everything happened all at once.

We saw a blue balloon drift into the room and burst, then we heard a loud explosion. The attic door slammed shut, and we heard a loud whistle and a reverberating bang. The bang seemed to come from the base of the floor. All this commotion seemed to propel the 'bhoo-jiis' into high gear. The now familiar rustling was accompanied by shrill squeaking. Multiple voices began shrieking downstairs.

We ran downstairs to see everyone crowded in the kitchen. There was half-cooked haleem everywhere. The pressure cooker had exploded, spewing its contents like a phirki on every surface of the kitchen—the stove, the floor, and a healthy glob of our dinner was even stuck to the ceiling.

Dad was looking sheepish, holding the lid of the now defunct pressure cooker. Rasheed Mammu's sweater was covered in splotches of haleem. Sharfu Chacha, who had come in from the back door, took one look and turned right back around, closing the door behind him.

While Rukhsana Mammi and Qamar Khala grabbed a few rags and started to help with the cleanup, Wasif and I beat a quick retreat to the living room where Nani was rubbing the sleep from her eyes. 'What's all the commotion?' she asked, and then stifling another yawn, asked, 'What's for dinner?'

'Probably Maggi,' I ventured.

CHAPTER 9

December 23: Mission Morrison's

'How are we going to pull it off?' whispered Wasif.

'Watch and learn,' I said, though I had literally no idea how we were supposed to pull this off.

'Well, the gut does house 4,500 different types of bacteria, so maybe we will be okay?'

Thanks Vali, the voice of doom in all our exciting (yet to happen) adventures.

The day's plan was to somehow reach Morrison's for their legendary kheema patties and cream puffs. 'Also, pani puri,' said Sehar.

'Not sure eating street food is a good idea,' said Urooj.

'Not for you firang types, but some of us have stomachs of steel,' scoffed Sehar.

Right, but how does a steel stomach meet street food while we are being chaperoned by Rasheed Mammu? We were discussing this while sitting in the Ambassador, trying to come up with a foolproof plan that involved eating out (not approved) while on an outing (triple approved).

'All set?' asked Rasheed Mammu.

'Are we all headed to the bazaar?' asked Urooj. 'We need some wool and beads.'

'What are you two making?' he asked.

'A blingy woolly mammoth?' guessed Wasif.

'Ah, well I could drop you off at the market on Mall Road while I gather the groceries and other supplies. There is a nature trail right near Mall Road,' he suggested.

'Or we could go to the Motilal Nehru Central State Library,' said Vali eagerly.

We all turned to look at him.

'Brilliant! I mean, yes, we can just hang out at the library. Right, Wasif?' I said, nudging him.

'What, a lib . . . oh yes, I mean we can look for more information on Jin . . . I mean, the history of Solan,' he said, unconvincingly.

'Wonderful. After the library, we can go for a hike and meet you back at the head of the trail,' I said.

'All right then, library and a hike it is!' said Rasheed Mammu as he tried to start the car. It whirred to life on the third try.

We drove past the mushroom roundabout on Mall Road and Mammu dropped us off at the entrance to the library. Much to Vali's disappointment, we didn't venture indoors. Thanks to Sehar's now-functioning phone, we GPS-ed our way through Mall Road. Ultimately, the smell of freshly baked bread was a better guide to get us right up to the doors of Morrison's Bakery.

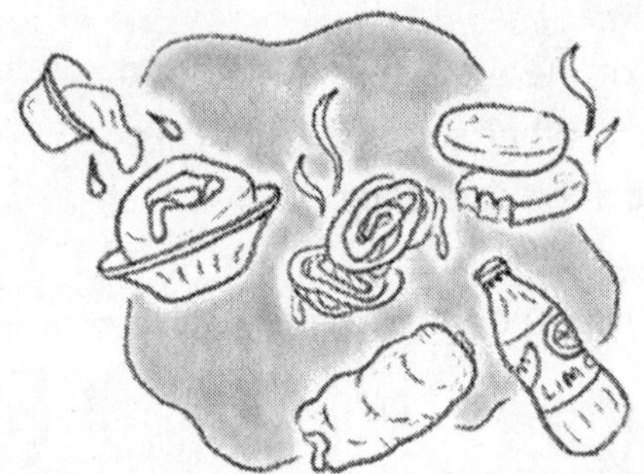

We polished off multiple plates of kheema patties and about a dozen cream puffs between the six of us. Sehar, who was still hankering for something chatpatta, dragged us all over to a thelewala to eat some spicy pani puri. And samosas. And piping hot jalebis. Then, Wasif, Vali and I decided to get some of the special nimbu soda. Wasif and I had great fun creating our own version of a game show— 'Kiski Dakaar Sab Se Tez?' Vali, of course, was tutting in a corner, pretending he didn't know us. With full bellies, we ambled to the head of the trail.

Rasheed Mammu showed up a little while later. He waved us over. 'Let's go grab some kheema patties and cream puffs to take home,' he said.

'Huh? Is that okay for everyone at home?' asked Urooj.

'Of course, it's practically a family tradition,' he answered.

'Oh, I see,' said Urooj glaring at us.

I didn't see why this was not a great situation. 'Hey, this is like icing sugar on the cream puff.'

A small voice said, 'Maybe we should just go home. I don't feel so good.' And because I was usually at the receiving end of this, I steered everyone out of Sehar's way, as the contents of her molten steel stomach made contact with the wild fern.

After we reached home and got an earful about eating street food (without the family), the grown-ups sent Sehar to the upar wala kamra. 'Sneaking out to eat pani puri!' harrumphed Ammi.

'And to think we shared our midnight feast with them,' tutted Qamar Khala.

Rukhsana Mammi was just annoyed at being cheated out

of her share of Morrison's treats. Clearly displeased at our lack of adaab, they planned another trip into town—without us. Nana wanted to quiz us on our hike-not-taken. When even Vali couldn't answer Nana's questions about the trees along the hike, he informed us of a re-trek the next day.

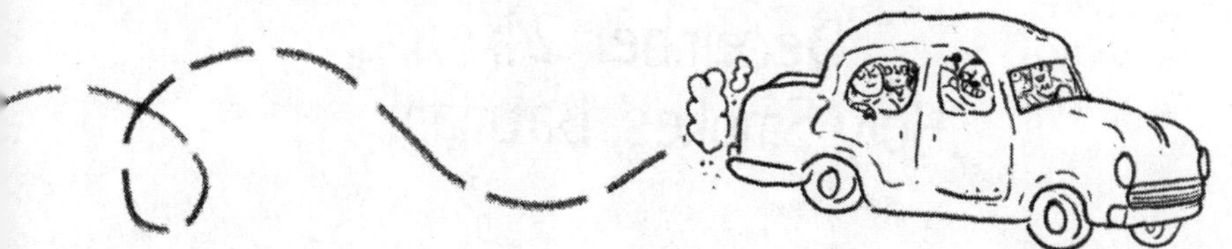

CHAPTER 10

December 24: Holy Smokes, Batman!

Early next morning, Nana led us out of the garden onto a winding path. It was so narrow that we had to walk in a single file. 'Stay in a straight line,' he called out as we walked ahead. 'Don't try and run, Wasif and Tanaaz,' he warned. 'This is a steep hillside.' A quick peek to my right and the long way down the hill made sure we were all doing our very best to stay in a very straight line.

Once the path got a bit wider, we saw a structure ahead. It looked like a little house. 'There's a baori here,' said Nana. 'My grandfather built this.' He pointed to what looked like a mini stepwell. Water was gushing out of an opening carved

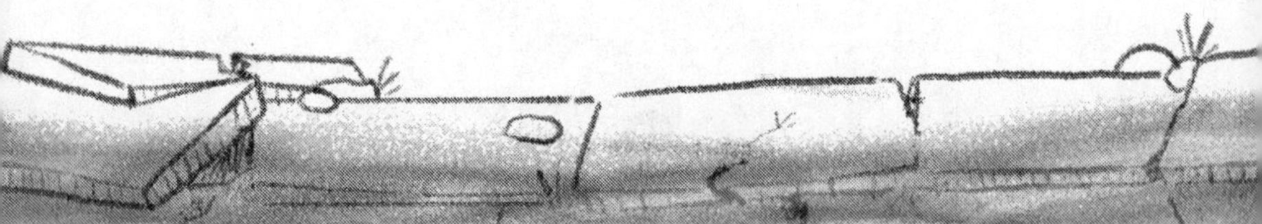

into the stone. It collected into the stepwell, and flowed out through an opening into a rectangular channel.

'Is this groundwater?' asked Vali.

'It used to be the only drinking water for miles,' said Nana. 'My mother would send us there with a gagar to collect water and take it to the house.' He cupped his hands into the channel and drank the water.

'Try it.' He motioned for us to do the same. We all dipped our hands into the water. So cold! We sipped it and it was cool, fresh and sweet. Nothing like any water we had tasted. 'Fill those tanks!' Nana laughed, patting his stomach. 'We have a long walk ahead!'

Vali was staring at one of the baori walls. He whispered, 'Look here.' He pointed to a picture carved into the stone. A fierce two-headed creature, with sharp claws, horns on its heads and pointy incisors stared back at us. 'Baoris sometimes have spirits residing in them,' he informed us.

'Is that what Sharfu Chacha means when he says jinn?' Urooj asked, her voice quaking a little.

'He also said jinn are shape-shifters,' added Vali.

'Meaning what?' I asked.

'That they can take the shape of anything. Or anyone,' Vali explained. We all gulped.

Wonderful, now we had a face, rather two, of a shape-shifting jinn to pair with the noises from the attic.

When we came back to the house, sore and red-nosed, Sehar was literally bouncing off of the walls. Clearly, sleeping in had welded back her stomach of steel.

'You won't believe what I saw.' Sehar practically yanked my arm off its socket.

'Ow! Not now, Sehar,' I said, bone-tired.

'Yes, right now,' she insisted. 'I know who, or rather what, the boo-ji is.' She smiled conspiratorially.

'Unfortunately, so do we,' said Urooj, showing her a picture of the two-faced jinn on her cell phone.

'What? No, that is not it, whatever that is. I saw it,' Sehar said.

'You went up to the attic?' said a shocked Vali.

'No, why would I do that, when I have other ways to find things out,' she said, yanking out her phone and opening up a video along with her commentary. 'I was trying to sleep but couldn't. So, then I had to call Dia and Arti, right? But there is literally no CPR here so I went to the terrace.

'Not only was my tummy upset but it was so cold! But hey, I figured, I should show people the real me, not just the fun parts, right? The only thing that would make it all better was to make a reel. So, I straightened my monkey cap, and adjusted the silver pompom to frame my face. I took a couple of selfies but the view wasn't so great, so I climbed up the bamboo ladder and sat on the parapet.

'I was trying to get my left profile when I saw something move in the attic window. I focused and zoomed with my phone and saw Omair Mammu in his monkey cap with the orange pompom. He was carefully perched on the open attic window, and seemed to be holding a little blanket.' She looked at all of us triumphantly at the end of her monologue as the rest of us squinted at the picture on her phone.

'Mammu has a puppy!' Urooj exclaimed.

'How do you know it is a puppy? It's just a teeny tiny black nose, which you've had to zoom 3x times to see,' pointed out Wasif.

'Nana would never allow pets in the house,' I said.

'Which is why they are hiding it,' Sehar whispered.

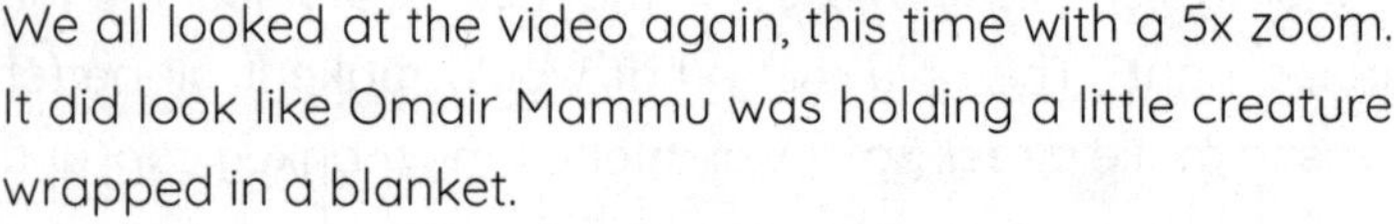

We all looked at the video again, this time with a 5x zoom. It did look like Omair Mammu was holding a little creature wrapped in a blanket.

'We have to ask him!' ventured Vali.

Just then we heard the attic door open and footsteps shuffling down the narrow staircase. We all rushed to the landing.

'We know what you have up there, Mammu!' announced Sehar.

‘Huh?’ came a muffled sound.

‘Sehar saw you by the attic window with a puppy. Tell us now or we’ll let Nana know!’ said Wasif, sounding mildly threatening.

‘I can come over to kulfi. Oh kulfi . . . Kufri . . . same-same,’ came the unmistakable voice of Omair Mammu. He walked up the stairs on the first floor. We all gasped!

‘But you are Omair Mammu!’ said Urooj, pointing to the unknown mammu in his sweater and monkey hat with the orange pompom.

‘Shape-shifter! Boo-jinn!!’ shouted Vali.

We all screamed.

‘Shh! Shh!’ said the unknown mammu, as he removed his monkey hat to show us a face covered with a medical face mask.

‘Aaarrgh!’ we screamed once more.

‘Quiet!’ he said taking off the mask to reveal the distressed face of Rasheed Mammu.

‘But the monkey cap with the orange pompom is Omair Mammu’s,’ said Urooj, unhappy at the thought of others willy-nilly changing around her colour-coded pompoms.

‘I just grabbed whatever I could find in the basket near the kitchen door,’ admitted Rasheed Mammu. ‘The attic gets cold.’

‘Is that why you were basking it in the sun?’ I asked.

‘It?’ repeated Rasheed Mammu.

‘The puppy!’ we all said all at once.

Omair Mammu and Rasheed Mammu exchanged a knowing glance.

‘We want to see it! Or we tell Nana, and you know his rules,’ Wasif doubled down.

‘Okay, we will go up quietly, but you all have to promise that what happens in the attic stays in the attic. No mentions of it to anyone else in the house. Not your parents. Not Nana, Nani. Not Sharfu Chacha. NO ONE,’ said Rasheed Mammu, now sounding moderately threatening. 'Or no more trips to Morrison's. Or anywhere else. Also, no talking. At all.'

We all pinky-swore to never tell. Rasheed Mammu did an about-turn on the stairs and reminded us to be very, very quiet. We all followed, the stairs creaking with the weight of six excited cousins looking forward to meeting a puppy! Omair Mammu followed behind us as we entered the narrow opening.

'Wait,' Rasheed Mammu cautioned us. 'Wear these,' he said, handing out some face masks.

In an empty space, no bigger than the size of our room below, we saw wooden rafters and creaky wooden boards. The attic wasn't insulated. It was freezing. Some sunlight drifted in from the window but, other than that, it looked like a very cold, dusty unused space. In the sunlight was a small upturned wire basket. We rushed to the basket that was lined with white towels at the bottom and a warm blanket. A small bowl of water was kept in a corner but there was no sight of a little pup.

'Where?' Vali mimed his hands in a question.

Omair Mammu whispered, 'Look up.'

We looked up to see a little brown ball cocooned onto itself. It hung from one of the wires of the basket with its claws and rocked back and forth. 'He loves rocking himself to sleep,' said Rasheed Mammu.

Possibly disturbed by the smells and commotion of six new visitors, the creature slowly opened up his wings to show himself. Six pairs of eyes peered into the gleaming eyes of a little bat.

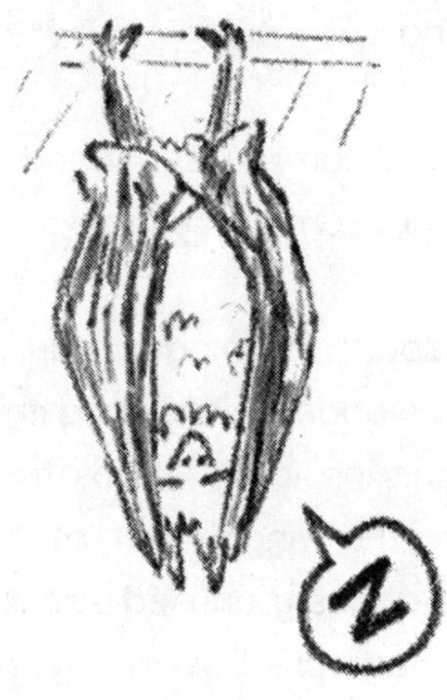

CHAPTER 11

December 25: Rocky Rules

1. NO TOUCHING. EVEN WITH GLOVES. OUR MAMMUS WILL DO ALL THE FEEDING AND CAREGIVING.
2. ALWAYS WEAR A MASK.
3. ONLY VISIT IN TWOS.
4. NO TALKING ABOUT BATS WITH ANYONE ELSE.

5. STRICT HAND-WASHING AFTER BEING IN THE ATTIC.
6. ONLY COME BY IN THE DAYTIME, WHEN ONE OF THE MAMMUS IS PRESENT.
7. ABSOLUTELY NO GOING UP TO THE ATTIC AT NIGHT.
8. NO BAT JOKES.

'Come on,' I said, 'that is totally not
fair. We can't have a bat in the house and not even crack a joke!'

Of course we had pinky-sworn to all these rules, but for once, rules didn't dampen our enthusiasm for being around Rocky. He was tiny, about the size of Mammu's palm.

'We found him in one of the bushes in the orchard about five weeks ago,' Rasheed Mammu told us.

'He was a frightened little thing. We see a lot of bats in the orchards during the summers,' said Omair Mammu.

'Oh, it's a flying fox!' said Vali triumphantly.

'No, it's called a pipette,' said Omair Mammu.

‘Pipistrelle,’ Rasheed Mammu corrected. ‘This year, summer was warmer than usual and with global warming, the bats are breeding later. He would have been hanging around his mother, learning to fly, and must have fallen down. It would have been too hard for his mother to carry him and fly up again.’

‘Poor baby,’ Urooj and Sehar said together.

‘I have a friend who works in wildlife conservation, but he has been away. I trained with him one summer, you know, when I was learning to drive too. He advised me to move the bat indoors and helped me with supplies to feed and take care of Rocky,’ he continued. ‘He watched him on video calls to monitor his progress and advised me how best to take care of him.’

‘Wait, our Rocky has been on screen?’ I asked, and no one took the bait. ‘What? This is a Rocky joke!’

Rocky, for his part, seemed mildly amused by all the attention. We watched as Omair Mammu began feeding him. He pulled out a small dish and added some mealworms from a can. He laid out a towel and Rocky crawled slowly towards the dish. He perched on the edge of the dish and gobbled the live worms with enthusiasm. Sometimes, he would even hold a particularly fat worm in his claws and chomp on it. His face looked like a little stuffed squirrel! His little pink tongue flicked out to lick his little lips.

'Pipistrelles mainly eat insects. He needs to be fed every couple of hours. It helps that he sleeps most of the day. And of course . . . ' Rasheed Mammu stopped short of telling us what we already knew.

'He's up at night!' exclaimed Vali.

'We leave him out of the basket so he can stretch his wings, get comfortable flying about on his own. He bumped his nose a couple of times, flying into the wall, but he is getting stronger,' said Omair Mammu.

'Suresh will be back in Solan soon. He plans to take Rocky with him to the rescue centre in Chandigarh. There he can learn to socialize with other bats and eventually be let back out into the wild,' said Rasheed Mammu.

'Aww,' squealed Urooj, 'he is so cute!' Wrapped up in a little warm towel to corral his wings and with only his little head peeking out and his triangular blunt black ears wiggling, he did look rather sweet. Of course, I thought otherwise when he bared his tiny teeth for his feeding sessions.

'Urooj, let's knit him a nice warm

blanket!' said Sehar, who could barely knit her brows together.

'What do you think is his favourite colour?' asked Urooj.

'Yellow—everyone knows that's the colour of the bat signal!' I exclaimed loudly.

The rest of the day was business as usual. We were shepherded to target practice and made our way to the terrace later in the day. We took turns with Omair Mammu and Rasheed Mammu checking in on Rocky. We found little bits and bobs to hang from his basket for him to play with. Urooj even made him a little yellow pompom ball that he loved to push back and forth.

At night, we were full of anticipation. We heard excited chirps and rustling as Rocky moved about, no doubt banging into the wall a few times. There never was a sweeter (and less scary) sound!

CHAPTER 12

December 26: Family Time

'What's this?' said Sehar as she pulled out a large black book. She pointed her flashlight at the book in the dark room, lit by a few candles and a kerosene lantern in the corner. It said 'Memories' in large gold letters on the spine.

'Oh, that's our old album,' said Qamar Khala.

'That was in our dresser upstairs,' said Nani.

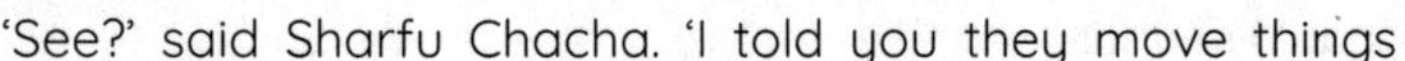

'See?' said Sharfu Chacha. 'I told you they move things

around.' he said, shaking his head and drawing his blanket closer. This time we all had to stifle our giggles.

'Who are these people?' said Wasif, flipping through the album. 'Nani! There is a picture of you with a crazy hairdo! Your hair is as tall as a building!' he laughed.

'It was all the rage! Beehive, they called it. Back in the day,' said Nani.

We all gathered around the album, leafing through the black-and-white pictures (there were a few colour ones at the end). Another picture of our grandparents popped up. Nana was wearing a stylish suit and Nani wore cat-eye sunglasses. 'You guys looked uber-cool!' said Urooj.

'And who are these stylish people, Ammi? And that ugly baby?' asked Sehar. Ammi looked at the picture in which a couple of ladies dressed in saris were sitting around on what looked like Nana and Nani's terrace many moons ago. She pointed, 'That's me and Qamar Khala and that ugly baby is you.'

Guffaws exploded around the room, much to Sehar's annoyance. In the dark of the night and with no electricity, we all gathered around the big fireplace in the living room. In the soft glow of the fire, Urooj and Sehar were knitting a bright yellow blanket. Rukhsana Mammi had made her special version of hot chocolate, which tasted literally like melted chocolate bars. Not that we were complaining!

'Who are these?' asked Urooj, pointing to two moustachioed men dressed in cricket gear with unruly mops of hair.

'Those are your mammus!' laughed Ammi.

'What? We look different with hair,' said Rasheed Mammu defensively.

'They sure know how to handle a bat,' I said, which earned me a few laughs and a raised eyebrow from Omair Mammu.

'That was when the two of you picked up a stray cat from the cricket grounds and tried to hide it from Baba,' laughed Qamar Khala.

'Some things don't change,' Omair Mammu said, winking at Rasheed Mammu, who smiled.

'Well, Baba does have a thing about rules and order . . . ' said Ammi.

'Even alphabetical order!' Qamar Khala, Rasheed Mammu, Ammi and Omair Mammu said together and burst out in peals of laughter.

'Wait, what's the joke?' I said, 'I don't get it.'

‘Haven’t you kids figured it out by now?’ asked Rukhsana Mammi.

‘Figured out what?’ asked Wasif, perplexed.

‘Nana’s name is Muneer, Nani’s name is Nazneen . . . ’ began Rasheed Mammu.

‘Oh, I get it!’ said Vali. ‘Omair Mammu is the oldest, then Parveen, Qamar and Rasheed!’

‘Wow! So, then me—Sehar, then Tanaaz!’ said Sehar.

‘Urooj, Vali, Wasif and Xenia!’ exclaimed Wasif.

‘That is actually pretty cool!’ I said.

Xenia and Nana were wrapped up in a blanket on Nana’s massive rocking chair. Her almost life-sized unicorn (um, if unicorns were real) was next to them. Xenia was nestled in the crook of his neck and their breaths slowly rose and fell in unison. I suspect Nana might actually decide to make a trip to Bangalore to see her soon.

Over cups of coffee, the adults continued to reminisce about their younger (and hairier) days. Wasif looked out into the dark night and then up at the ceiling and said, 'I am the darkness, I am the night,' in his best raspy Batman imitation.

'Well, maybe we wouldn't be stuck in the dark if we had bat-teries,' I laughed.

A batty family and a real-life bat—this had been a great holiday!

CHAPTER 13

December 27: A Flying Start

'Remember everyone, play it cool,' I said.

'Act normal,' added Wasif.

'But it's D-day!' said Vali, skipping down the stairs.

We were ready. But no one at home could know.

Urooj and Sehar had already speed-knitted Rocky's yellow blanket and given it to Rasheed Mammu. He laid it at the bottom of Rocky's wire basket and wrapped him tight. Rocky's little head was poking out and he looked on interestedly at the flurry of activity. Rasheed Mammu's friend was coming by to pick Rocky up today.

The sun peeked out of the sky, turning it bright blue, which meant Nani had us marching back to the cabin for target practice. Even though she now let us use the bows, I can't say we were making that much progress. Nani was worse.

'We really have to get her to wear her glasses,' said Vali, who was in charge of picking up all the fallen arrows. Some had made their way many trees over.

'We are working on it,' winked Urooj, and Sehar elbow-bumped her.

We trudged back home and straight up to the terrace to get some sun. We collapsed on the charpoys and Ammi, Qamar Khala and Rukhsana Mammi got to work massaging warm mustard oil on our sore shoulders and arms. The sun felt good on our faces and we began to relax. Sharfu Chacha brought out steaming cups of chai and milk. I was warm and drowsy as I lay flat on the charpoy looking at the sky. Suddenly, something caught the corner of my eye. Something had whizzed past the window.

I sat straight up.

'Where are Omair Mammu and Rasheed Mammu?' I asked.

'Storeroom.'

'Study.'

Both answers came at once.

'Let's go,' I motioned to the others. Wasif and Vali needed no prompting but Sehar and Urooj seemed reluctant to leave their spot in the sun.

'Why? What's the rush?' yawned Sehar.

'Holy smokes, Batman!' I said urgently. They look puzzled. Well, that flew right over their heads. Gah, no time to waste right now.

'Vali, get Rasheed Mammu. We'll find Omair Mammu!' I said, as we ran down the stairs.

Wasif and I went past Sharfu Chacha, who cautioned us to slow down, all the way to the storeroom where Omair Mammu was looking for the mealworms.

'He's doing it! He's flying!' we yelled.

'Wait what? I just left him out of his basket while I got

the worms...' said Omair Mammu, tossing the can into a wicker tray.

We all ran into the house and to the stairs, where we were joined by a confused Rasheed Mammu and Vali. We bounded up the stairs and ran straight into Nana and Xenia.

'What's the rush?' asked Nana.

'Flying Bat!' I blurted out.

'What, rat? I thought you took care of that, Rasheed,' asked Nana.

'Oh err . . . um . . . yes, in fact, Suresh—you remember him—he's a wildlife biologist now, he's coming by today to . . .' stammered a nervous Rasheed Mammu.

'Ophthalmologist? Why do you need an eye doctor . . . '

began Nana quizzically. Fortunately, Xenia succeeded in pulling him down the stairs, much to our mammus' relief.

We rushed up the stairs to the attic. A monkey-capped and masked Omair Mammu carefully opened the door and peeked inside. He let us in, one by one. 'Chhiirrup,' said Rocky in a happy way.

'Hello Rocky,' said Vali. 'Chiirrupp,' Rocky said again and opened up his wings. He flew across the room to the rafter near the window.

We all broke out into cheers of delight. Rocky, not wanting to disappoint his audience, did it again and again. A thrilled Rasheed Mammu wore his gloves and beckoned him. He flew gracefully and perched himself upside down on his finger.

'I suppose this means you are ready, little guy,' he said in a quiet whisper. Soon after, Mammu's friend called to say he would be there in twenty minutes. It was time to begin Operation Exit. Or more like Operation Exit-the-house-without-being-noticed-with-a-bat.

Wasif and I stationed ourselves at the landing downstairs to give the all-clear. Vali had to keep Ammi and the other aunts at bay, and Urooj and Sehar had to make sure Nana and Nani were busy and away from the front door. Rasheed Mammu snuck his friend into the house. Suresh Uncle was tall and lanky. His hair bounced up and down as he bounded up the stairs all the way to the attic.

Soon, they came down again with a loosely draped towel around Rocky's basket. All clear! We managed to sneak down the stairs and get to the car when someone said, 'Kahan chale?'

Sharfu Chacha! We had forgotten about him.

'Oh, er, just going out for a spin,' said Omair Mammu.

'What's this?' Sharfu Chacha asked, coming closer and peering inside the basket.

'Oh, we caught him in the attic—Suresh is taking him to . . .' said Rasheed Mammu hurriedly.

'A rat! Good grief, what are you doing with a rat?' he practically shrieked, possibly now alerting everyone in the house. 'Bibiji, this is really it, I quit!'

We bundled up Rocky and Suresh Uncle into his car and said our speedy goodbyes before Sharfu Chacha returned with our whole clan in tow. That was a close call.

Later that day, Suresh Uncle sent us videos of Rocky's debut at the rescue centre. It was a squat, peeling yellow bungalow. Well, at least the yellow was a good sign.

He trained the camera on all the other animals at the centre. We saw dogs and cats, even a stray pheasant! Suresh Uncle walked on with Rocky in his basket to an old cabin. Past the door was an open room separated by netting and full of bats! 'These are the adult colonies. Once Rocky is ready, we can introduce him to the others. Once he acclimatizes to other bats, that can increase his chance of survival in the wild,' he explained in the video.

He took the basket and opened it on the other side of the netting. Rocky shot out like a bolt of lightning! He found a spot in the corner and watched the other bats. 'It will take him a while to adjust to them and for them to adjust to him as well. He's flying great! He looks strong and is curious about the others. He should fit in in no time,' Suresh Uncle assured us.

We watched Rocky take to his new surroundings many times that night on our phone screens. The house was eerily quiet. No rustling, no chirping. No boo-jis for us tonight. It felt a little bit bittersweet.

CHAPTER 14

December 28: Bouncy Castles and Flying Tea Cosies

All was quiet in the Rizvi house. Nothing was stirring, not even a mouse. Or, well, a bat.

We must have slept in till nine in the morning. How did that happen? I remembered that Rocky had moved on to other adventures. I looked up at the ceiling and the familiar

rustling was no longer heard. I think I felt a pang, missing the little scares we had from Rocky's flying lessons.

At breakfast, Sehar and Urooj kept whispering conspiratorially, leading me to think they were plotting something again. Wasif was subdued though Vali was jabbering away about bats and colonies and how young bats train with older ones. 'Also, pipistrelle bats are like a natural pest control with all the insects they eat,' he informed us.

Even with the sunshine, we didn't feel like loitering on the terrace with the rest of the family. Wasif nudged me and said, 'Should we go upstairs?'

I looked askance. 'There are rules. We aren't allowed,' I said.

'Correction, we *weren't* allowed,' he clarified.

We walked up the narrow landing and gently pushed open the attic door. We stepped inside and it felt cold even with the sun streaming in through the window. Omair Mammu had pretty much removed any signs that Rocky was ever here, which made us a little sad.

'Nothing to see here,' said Wasif.

'Ya, no. Nothing except Xenia's head bobbing up by the window,' I said.

'What?!' We both looked at each other and then rushed to the window to see Xenia's head, and the rest of her, bobbing up and down a huge bouncy castle. Boy, did this girl have Nana wrapped around her finger! We peeped through the window to see the whole family gathered below. You didn't have to ask us twice. We raced down the stairs and out to the terrace.

There was an almost six-foot-tall bouncy castle in the middle of the terrace. It had bright pink and purple towers on all four sides, and was covered with pictures of unicorns and rainbows. It looked like the most vile thing on the planet. We couldn't wait to try it out!

Sehar, Urooj, Vali and Xenia were already in the castle, taking selfies mid-jump. We got in and joined in the general mayhem. Nana was laughing uproariously at our antics. Wasif was trying to do back flips, which earned him an earful from his mother.

Dad, Qaisar Khalu, Omair Mammu and Rasheed Mammu showed up too, abandoning their posts in the sun. Soon enough, they demanded the kids give them a turn. 'This is the most excited we've seen them,' Ammi quipped. 'You had better give them a go!'

PUSH, KIDS!

They scrambled in, trying to outdo each other's high jumps. Sharfu Chacha showed up with chai, hot chocolate and a heaped mountain of boiled peanuts. 'Oh dear, I forgot the tea cosy,' he mumbled. 'Rukhsana Bhabhi, can you grab the tea cosy on your way up, please?'

Rukhsana Mammi showed up with a floral embroidered tea cosy. 'Here, catch,' she said, throwing it in Sharfu Chacha's direction. Only it was intercepted midway in a graceful swoop by Nani. She was all smiles as she passed the tea cosy to Sharfu Chacha. Her glasses glinted in the sun.

'Glasses? Now how on earth did anyone convince her to wear her glasses?' Qamar Khala asked.

'We did!' shouted Sehar and Urooj together.

They ran to give Nani a hug and dragged her, laughing and screaming, to the rest of us. Ammi noticed that Nani's glasses were held up by a bedazzled chain which had a mix of magnetic beads and crochet thread. So this is what they had been working on!

In the warm winter sun, surrounded by my quirky family with a huge bouncy castle, and the echoing laughter of uncles and aunts and cousins (minus the chirps of a little bat), this felt like the best family holiday we could have had!

ACKNOWLEDGEMENTS

A book may be written by one person, but there are a lot of people who contribute to the back story. To my entourage, with heartfelt gratitude:

To Niyati Awasthi for regaling me with your childhood antics during Shimla winters.

To Kanika Mall for sharing your stories of Solan.

To Rakhi Basu for your lightning-fast research chops and for willing to listen to me moan and groan for over 30 years and counting. There's more where that came from!

To Rohit Chakravarty for great conversations and gentle corrections about wildlife in the Himalayas.

To my editor Aparna Kapur for having faith in me, and using your sharp insights to steer me away from self-sabotage.

Tah-e-dil se shukriya to my batty family . . .

To my parents for their never-ending supply of Urdu phrases which the rest of us may or may not understand.

To Baba, for reading everything I write.

To my brothers Tabish and Taru for all things funny, silly and quirky.

To my Bhabhi, better known as Mehnaz Mammijaan, for fielding legal questions.

And finally, to my little circle of love and endless amusement, I can't thank you enough.

Atif for being my first reader and being honest about my work, Arham for all your sincere duas and Aamna our little sparkler of joy.

And thank you, dear reader, for picking up this book.

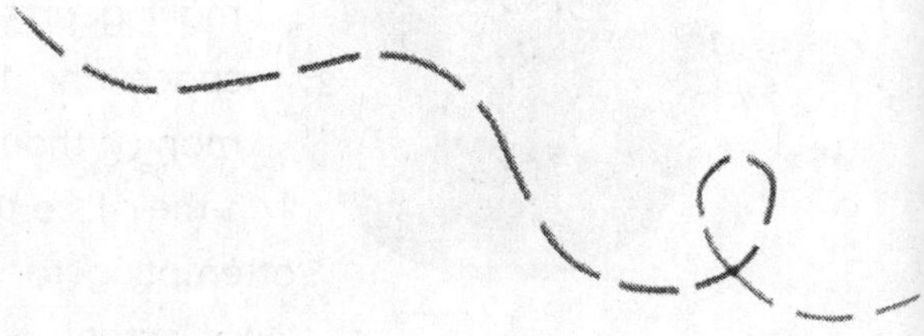

ABOUT THE AUTHOR

Sadaf Siddique is an author and editor. She is partial to puns, peacocks, parathas and alliteration. She loves spinning stories and nonsensical rhymes. Her focus on innovative ideas for social change led to the Counter Islamophobia Through Stories campaign. Her books include *Muslims in Story*, *My Street* and *Hakeem's Hiccups*.

ABOUT THE ILLUSTRATOR

Riya is an illustrator and comic artist from Chennai. They love making art about cats, queers, space and the (sometimes too many!) thoughts in their head. In their free time you'll find them attempting to befriend stray cats, cooking instant noodles at midnight, and worrying about the world.